Get
Up
Woman

INSPIRATIONS FOR A WOMAN WITH AUTHORITY

BY LESEDI MAMATELA

Enlightened Christian Gathering (ECG) Church
Tshwane Events Centre, Hall H
205 Soutter Street
Pretoria
0117

This book and other titles are available at ECG, Pretoria branch.

ISBN 978-0-9947109-2-5

For more information, contact Shepherd Bushiri Publishers:
info@sbpublishers.org

Contents

Foreword

There is a saying, "A woman's work is never done." As a mother, you can never be too sure if your efforts quite hit the mark. It is when you see your work, mission and love replicated in your daughters that you know that heaven is smiling on you! I am so proud to be a chapter in this book and to play a part in this testimony. It warms my heart and elates my spirit to know that this generation is responding to God's Word, as the prophets of old said. Be blessed by this eloquent offering, as I have been.

With Love,
Prophetess Mary Bushiri

Dedication

I dedicate this book to my spiritual parents, Prophet Shepherd Bushiri and Prophetess Mary Bushiri, who inspire me. I also dedicate this book to my biological parents, David Mamatela and Cathrine Mamatela, as well as my sister, Realeboga Mamatela, who fill my life with joy. I am grateful to God for bringing us together as a family and for showing me that I am blessed through this said union.

Last, but not least, I dedicate this book to God; without Him producing this work would not be possible.

Acknowledgements

In this book, I offer many stories shared with me by friends, family, and people I have met around the world. I appreciate and acknowledge their contributions and support.

I offer special thanks to my spiritual father, who installed the desire and passion to share with others whom God has deposited in me.

Introduction

When God created women, He knew that they would be a precious gift to the world. Women are very rare beings that cannot be explained or described by mere or ordinary words. They are intelligent, powerful, talented, creative, compassionate, and according to the Bible, equal to men.

In this book, I remind women of the authority that God Almighty has given them. In Genesis 1:26 the Bible says, *"Then God said, 'Let us make mankind in our image, in our likeness, so that they may rule over the fish in the sea and the birds in the sky, over the livestock and all the wild animals, and over all the creatures that move along the ground'."*

In the Scripture above, God created both male and female. Creation happened to both at the same time, but it is only in Genesis Chapter 2, where God first formed Adam and then came Eve. Creation and formation, therefore, are two very distinct operations. When we talk about creation, we refer to the process whereby something is put into a framework that does not necessarily involve the physical. Formation, on the other hand, is bringing into manifestation that which is from the unseen world. The only difference between male and female is the womb. Hence, the name woman. A woman is a man with a womb, meaning you can achieve what a man can achieve and even do greater things.

If you are reading this book, then you should know that you are a woman who has been given authority by the highest God, and it is time for you to exercise this authority.

God created women, and He said that everything He created was good. When God created you in His image, He put a part of Himself in you. Our God is a God of authority, at His name every knee bows down, and every tongue confesses that He is Lord. He spoke words into existence and made the stars; He made you out of dust and breathed life into you. God is your Heavenly Father, and you have the same DNA as Him. This means you have the same authority God has. Can you take a moment to imagine what you are capable of doing? You are destined to do great things in life, destined to leave your mark on this generation. The devil is troubled every time he thinks about you. You are a great person.

God has a wonderful plan for your life, and I pray and trust that reading this book, will help you make progress on your journey towards a confident life filled with love, laughter, and authority.

Lesedi Mamatela

Chapter 1

Isaiah 43: 3-4 - *"For I am the Lord your God, the Holy One of Israel, your Saviour; I give Egypt for your ransom, Cush and Seba in your stead. Since you are precious and honoured in my sight and because I love you, I will give people in exchange for you, nations in exchange for your life."*

In the Scripture above, God was reminding the Israelites of how valuable they are to Him. Israel would not walk in God's ways, and when He corrected them for their disobedience, they were stubborn and resisted God's rebuke. One would think that it should have followed that God would abandon and destroy them, but no, God continued with His love and care for His people. God purchased them dearly because He knew how valuable they are. God was willing to give Egypt away in their stead because they were so dear to Him.

It is of paramount importance, therefore, that you take a few minutes and look into your heart. How do you feel about yourself? Is your answer in agreement with God's Word? The very word that states that you are the apple of His eye. Chosen people. A holy nation? Do you believe that you are wonderfully and fearfully made? If not, I encourage you to study the Word of God, and you will find out that you are precious in His sight; you are a jewel, created in your mother's womb by God's hand.

Your background is not ordinary; you came from the best. It does not matter what you may look like. It does not matter how many weaknesses you have or addictions you struggle with. You may have made some mistakes like what I did, but what overthrows all of that is that, inside of you is the DNA of the Almighty God. You come from a bloodline of winners, overcomers and champions.

If you would study your spiritual bloodline, you will see how our ancestor Esther stepped up and saved her people from death. The king had ordered that every Jew be killed, but Esther would not have that. The Bible says she chose, instead, to go before the king and plead for her people to be spared. This was a dangerous thing to do because no one was to go before the king without being called. However, Esther showed courage and went to the king despite all odds (Esther 5-10). You have the same DNA as her, which means, courage in your bloodline.

Deborah was the only female who judged Israel. God used Deborah to communicate His will to the people of Israel. God told her to send a man named Barak and say to him that the Lord commanded him to take 10000 men and go up to Mount Tabor. There, God would help Barak and the Israelites defeat Sisera. Sisera also is known as the commander of the Canaanite army had been oppressing Israel for years (Judges 4). Israel defeated Sisera, which shows there is an increase and promotion
in   your   bloodline.

Hannah, although barren, never gave up hope that God would hear her prayer (1 Samuel 1). That is a sign that great faith is in your bloodline. David, a shepherd boy, defeated a giant, Goliath (1 Samuel 17) and Samson pushed down the walls of a large building (Judges 16). There is favour, supernatural strength and power in your bloodline.

Do not underestimate yourself or think that you are not good enough or qualified for that career. Your bloodline is full of champions. You are only destined to win, overcome and live in victory. It does not matter what people may say about you or what your present circumstances look like. That addiction you struggle with is not permanent. The Scriptures say that where the Spirit of God is, there is freedom (2 Corinthians 3:17). Meaning, freedom is in your bloodline. That sickness is only temporary. The Word of God says that by His stripes, we are healed (Isaiah 53:5), not that we are going to be healed or still in the process of being healed.

Lack, struggle, and barely getting by are not your portion or part of your destiny. Abundance, prosperity and increase are part of your future. Apostle John says in 3 John 1:2 that he wishes above all things that we may prosper and be in good health just as our soul prospers.

When negative thoughts tell you that you are not going to make it, or it is never going to happen, keep checking what your spiritual birth certificate says about you. You have to remind yourself of who you are and most importantly, what God says about you. Your DNA is found in God's Word. You are not meant to live an average life, always getting the leftovers or borrowing. No, it says in Psalm 5:12, *"God's favour surrounds me like a shield."* It says, "I will lend and not borrow. Goodness and mercy are following me." That is what is in your DNA. The facts may change, but the truth – God's Word – always remains the same.

A few years ago, I spoke with a beautiful lady. She was telling me how she sees herself. What amazed me most was that her opinion about herself was based on what other people thought about her, and not whom God said she was. I must say she was gorgeous, but she did not know that. She let other people devalue her worth. I have realised that many people in life do not know who they are or have never been told who they are. They have had negative voices repeatedly playing in their lives. While I was speaking to her, I got this revelation. So, our body consists mainly of water, and when you look at water, you can see your reflection. Now, when God looks at you, He sees His reflection. God is beautiful. You are made in His image! Meaning, you are also beautiful and have His DNA.

Never let any person devalue your worth and tell you that you are not good enough or fit for that position. The one who created you sees Himself when He looks at you. You are not a mistake. Even if your parents have told you that they did not want you, I can assure God wanted you. It does not matter what people may think or say. If there is one thing, I have learned is that people can deliberate, people can discuss, people can even conclude your matter, but it is God who has the final say in your life. Therefore, take heart, and stop listening to what people say or think about you and your situation, only God has the final say about you. When thoughts tell you anything either than what the Word of God says, block out the negativity and focus on the Word of God. Do not get discouraged or grow weary; keep checking what your spiritual birth certificate says about you. Keep reminding yourself of who you are. Keep your head held up high. You are valuable, worthy, gifted, talented and have a purpose of fulfilling on this earth; you are a woman with authority. Stop listening to other people. No one can stop you. Get up, woman!

PRAYER

Dear God, thank You for reminding me that I am precious and valuable in Your sight. Thank You that You and I share the same DNA, which means that I do not come for an ordinary background and that I am only destined for great things. Please continue to work in me, so that I become all that You have created me to become, in Jesus' name, I pray. Amen.

Chapter 2

Value your time

Ephesians 5:16 - *"Making the most of every opportunity, because the days are evil."*

Paul tells us in Ephesians to make the most of every opportunity. The Amplified Version even states further on the same scripture, that we should live purposefully and accurately and not be vague and thoughtless. If you want to reach your highest potential and achieve your goals, you have to make sure you value your time. You should make sure that you are not distracted, going with the flow and waiting to see what happens, but you should be purposeful. Another version of the same scripture tells us to "redeem the time". That means that we should not waste time.

Time does fly and, in some situations, it may feel as if time crawls. You should always remember that each of us only has a certain amount of time on this earth. Woman, what are you doing with your time?

Time is one of the most valuable things that we have. It is more valuable than money. You can make more money, but you can never make more time. God gave us the gift of time, meaning we also have been given the responsibility by Him to use our time wisely. You need to realise that we are not always going to be here.

You should always ask yourself if you are living your life to the fullest with purpose and passion; or are you just doing whatever comes along and not being focused? Are you busy working on a career you do not like? Are you in a job you do not feel passionate about doing or spending time with people who only discourage you? That, woman, is called wasting your time. You should know you are either investing or wasting your time.

The first step to make sure you do not waste your time is to set goals. Set short term and long-term goals. Make sure you are working towards your goal every day. Ask yourself questions such as what would you want to achieve this week or this year? Where do you want to be ten years from now? You must write down your goals. Do not just go another year studying a career you do not like or doing something you are not passionate about. Life is flying by. This is your one chance. It is rare for one to get an opportunity to start afresh. We cannot go back and relive our twenties or thirties. We can never take back a day once it is over.

Make sure you know what you are doing with your time and where you are heading. As Apostle Paul says, make the most of each opportunity (Ephesians 5:16). Deciding to spend your time with a friend, who has no goals and is not going anywhere, is wasting your time. I, for one, can relate because I used to spend so much time with friends who were always going out and spending money. And when I say go out, I mean every weekend and sometimes during the week. Not only did I lose a lot of money, but I also lost much time investing in things that were not of benefit to me.

The scripture in Luke 2:36 – 38, talks about living well-spent lives. When we go to bed at night, we should ask ourselves, "Did I live a day that was spent well? Did I take steps to achieve my goals?"

I used to have a friend who was incredibly talented in tennis and had great potential, but she was not disciplined when it came to how she spent her time. She had excellent intentions but was quickly distracted by small things, such as missing practice because she wanted to go out partying or to see her boyfriend, and she ended up off-course. There are several good things one can give up one's time to. You have to be disciplined and learn to stay focused on what is best for you. If not, you will end up chasing the latest trend, trying to keep up with your friends, and in so doing, the dire consequence is the fact that you will lose your destiny.

I remember one year when I was still pursing my BCom. General Degree at the University of Pretoria; I always used to postpone studying a module that was giving me difficulty. I would always come up with excuses and say, "I'll study in one hour." As soon as I am about to study, a friend would call me, and we would discuss it for two hours. I will tell myself again, "I'll just study tomorrow." Tomorrow was always tomorrow, and the next thing I knew, I had procrastinated so much to the point that I failed the module, all because I was unable to use my time wisely, and I was not disciplined.

Stay focused! It is easy to get sidetracked by things that are not part of your destiny, and before you realise it, the day or year is gone. Nothing will be more frustrating than to come to the end of your life and think, "Why did I waste so many days and not achieve my goals?"

It is important to realise God has given you authority, first and foremost over your own life. He gave you the gift of time, but He also gave you the responsibility to use your time wisely. It is your responsibility to accept and exercise that authority, or else you may blame others for something you should be doing something about. You should make your own decisions according to what you believe God's will is for you. Remember that on Judgement Day, God will not ask anyone else to give an account for your life. He will ask you only.

A woman of authority understands that she needs to invest her time wisely to accomplish her goals. I have learned one valuable lesson in life, and that is with every decision you make; it is either blessings or consequences that will follow you. We are not always going to be here. The Scripture says, *"Our life is like a mist. We're here for a moment, and then we're gone"* (James 4:14). Make this decision with me today that you are going to be disciplined, not waste any more days and invest your time wisely.

The Scripture in Ecclesiastes 3:1 reminds us there is a time for everything. It says, *"To everything, there is a season, and a time to every purpose under the heaven."* Nothing is a surprise to God. God's timing is perfect. He is never early, never late, but just on time.

I believe it is essential to go through every season and not try to avoid or jump any seasons. There are things that if you miss, you have to go back to and pick up. There is a reason why you have to go through every season; God wants to teach you something.

The first university that I went to, I did not live like a student. I did not have any student friends; I was not attending any of the activities that were happening on campus, and being honest with you, I did not enjoy the student life. I was taking part in activities that should have been done by people who were working. Hence, I did not get the student results I wanted. I believe God let me re-do my entire university career again, at a new university, the University of Johannesburg, because there were valuables that I needed to gain in that specific season. And until I learnt something from that season, I would keep on repeating that season. My grandfather, Prophet Uebert Angel, said such a powerful statement that "There are stages in life that need to be experienced and graduated from otherwise you would need to revise your life for those stages to be dealt with."

As a woman of authority, you can trust God's timing. God has it all figured out. What you are praying about believing God for is not going to be one second late. God has already set the right time for everything. Just stay in peace; you do not have to worry. God has never put a time frame to His promises, but He will surely deliver. God directs your steps, and He is faithful to His Word.

The society that we live in usually wants everything to happen right now. The scriptures says, *"It's through faith and patience that we inherit the promises"* (Hebrews 6:12). Having faith is not always a problem, but you have to make sure you have patience too, or you will continue to try and figure things out, and that will only frustrate you. Remember, God is gracious and has His own way of working. His ways are not our ways.

My encouragement to you is to trust God and His perfect timing. Let Him be the one to define your purpose. He knows what He is doing. He only has great plans for you. No matter how much time He may take, know that He always has your best interest in heart. Believe me, when God brings you out of your situation, the whole world is not going to doubt that the God you serve is awesome and astonishing. Take courage, be still and know He alone is God.

PRAYER

Dear Lord, thank You for giving me the authority to be able to choose how I spend my time. Thank You for allowing me to redeem my time. Today, I choose to trust Your timing. Thank You that You have it all figured out. Please help me to value the time You have given me and to use it wisely, in Jesus' name, I pray. Amen.

CHAPTER 3

Choose your circle wisely

1 Samuel 16:7 *"But the LORD said to him, 'Pay no attention to how tall and handsome he is. I have rejected him because I do not judge as people judge. They look at outward appearance, but I look at the heart'."*

The Lord tells Samuel in the above Scripture that man sees the outside appearance, but the Lord sees what is within. As a woman of authority, who is made in the image of God, you need to learn to look beyond the exterior of people and see their heart. You need to know that you cannot just associate yourself with people who are not going anywhere, who are not focused, disciplined or have a goal they want to achieve. Such people compromise and take the easy way out, which is not something a woman of authority should be doing.

There is a saying that says, "You become the five people you spend the most time with." If you surround yourself with people who are jealous, bitter or unhappy, you will end up resentful, angry and unhappy. It is as the principle of sowing and reaping. You cannot sow a seed of apples and expect to reap oranges. The same principle applies to your friendships; if you choose to have mediocre friends, it will rub off on you. That is what it says in Proverbs: *"When you walk with wise men, you will become wise"* (Proverbs 13:20).

Woman have a look at the type of people who are surrounding your life. You are most likely to become like them in a few years. If you have friends that are successful, leaders and are consistently positive and focused, you are more than likely to inherit such great qualities. However, if you have friends that are continually speaking negative thoughts, that are undisciplined and do not have any set goals of where they would like to be or wish to achieve in life, then woman, I suggest that you go and find yourself a circle of new friends. You really cannot become whom God destined and created you to be while you still have those specific people in your life. They may be good people and even have good hearts, but your destiny and who God created you to be is far much greater, do not allow them to bring you down and leave you unfocused. The only thing that may be keeping some people from a new level of their destiny is wrong friendships. Woman learn to prune off some relationships that are not adding value to your life.

In 2016, when I first started my varsity career, I have to be very honest and admit that I had chosen the wrong friends. They were not bad people at all, as a matter of fact, we would always go to church together. However, the problem was that we were all at different phases in life. I was still a student, trying to get my degree, while they had finished their schooling or just sitting at home and practically doing nothing. It became a big problem because they were always available to go on outings as they had more free time on their hands. Then I would continuously give up my study time to hang around with people who were not motivated or even in the process of obtaining their degree. This had a direct contribution to me not doing well in school. I am not blaming them for my results, because at the end of the day, I chose them to be my friends, but they did have a contributing factor. Instead of me being at a certain level, which was a graduation, I was one step behind. It is essential to choose your friends wisely. You do not need some of these people in your life if you have a vision of where you would like to be in a few years from now.

One great person, who understood that He needed to be very selective with His friendships was Jesus. I am pretty sure that everyone desired to be close to Him, but Jesus only chose twelve disciples with whom He had spent most of His time on earth. Out of the those twelve, Jesus had an inner circle that He decided to be close too: Peter, James and John. Woman, be very careful whom you chose to allow into your inner circle, choose people who you can trust and be accountable to.

When you choose those two or three people you want to be close to, make sure they have your back, they are focused and are 110 per cent there for you. Have people that believe in you, that believe in your vision. Sometimes it happens that you are not seeing God's plans for your life because of certain people in your life. You are spending valuable time with people who were never meant to be in your life. Sometimes we know a person is not suitable for our lifestyle, or we know and feel it in our spirit that the person is not meant to be in our lives, but often we think letting him or her go is not an option because we will feel lonely. I know feeling lonely is not a good feeling, but one thing you should know is that feelings are only temporary. Know that when you choose to leave someone who is not taking you anywhere, God will always give you someone better and more deserving of you.

Sometimes you fail to hear the voice of God because of certain people in your life. For example, the story of Abram and Lot, in Genesis. Lot had to leave Abram's life for God to speak to Abram (Genesis 12-19). It was not that God was not speaking to Abram all that time, but he could not hear the voice of God because of a particular person in his life; he was too much congested and distracted. There are things that God could not do for Abram because he had certain people around him. Be wise; walk away and separate yourself from people who will drain your energy and destroy your potential. Some relationships are not worth it; neither are they healthy for your well-being.

Paul tells us in Romans 16:17 to watch out and keep away from those who cause "divisions". You may have people in your life that are causing you to go astray, dividing your focus and leading you away from God's plan or a simple example like mine where they were dividing my focus and causing me not to study anymore. Notice how Paul is not saying we should pray about it and ask God for direction. No, his instruction is plain and simple, "stay away from them". This means you need to go far away from them.

Ask God to give you something called "divine connections". Connections you know that come from only above, He will always choose people for you that you would not choose because unlike us He looks at the heart. Ask God also to help you leave and let go of people who are not meant to be in your life. Trust Him to bring the right people in your life; people who would have your back entirely and only want the best for you. Get Up woman and take authority over the type of friendships you have.

PRAYER

Dear God, thank You for giving me the authority to choose whom I can allow into my circle. I pray for divine connections; may You send the right people into my life and help me not to be like Abraham and keep a Lot in my life. Help me to let go of those who are not meant to be in my life, in Jesus' Mighty name. Amen.

CHAPTER 4

Confidence

2 Kings 18:5 - *"Hezekiah trusted in, leaned on, and was confident in the Lord. The God of Israel; so that neither after him nor before him was any one of all the kings of Judah like him."*

Hezekiah is one of my favourite kings in the Bible. He came to the throne after a long line of unrighteous rulers, who were worshipping idols. Hezekiah had a goal, and his goal was to turn the nation back to God where it belonged. He removed all the altars that were dedicated to idols. He refused to put his trust in idols. He was known as a man who had confidence in the Lord, who trusted God with all his heart.

I believe confidence is having complete faith in God. The king of faith that is strong and unshaken no matter what challenges may come your way. It is the kind of faith that you know with God's help you can achieve anything. With confidence, there is a reality, and we do not ignore that fact, but we have faith that He is still able to change our reality.

Through the years when I was still in high school, many people tried to hold me back from God's call on my life. There were those people who judged me falsely because they did not understand what I was doing and why I was doing it. There was a time when my friend Kea and I were praying for someone to receive her healing during our lunch break in high school; we were reported to the school office as some of the learners around felt uncomfortable and that we should not be sharing our spiritual belief with others. We were eventually banned from holding prayer sessions during our lunch break. I wanted to sit down and forget about my vision from God because of their criticism and judgement.

However, I knew that God called me; He was on my side had a big God sitting down, forgetting the vision that God gave me was not an option. He gave me the strength to go forward no matter what others thought because my confidence was in him. It was not always easy, but one thing I learnt from my experience is that it is better to go through all the opposition than to be out of the will of God and live a frustrated and unfulfilled life.

Today I can stand in front of my fellow students and tell them about the One who saved me. Had I not gone through those trials and tribulations; I do not think I would have been able to serve God in front of thousands today.

One thing about standing up that you should know is that it

does not mean that you should have an aggressive or rebellious attitude, especially towards those people who may not understand you. It simply means getting to the finish line with quiet inner confidence. It knows inside that despite what is happening on the outside; everything is going to be all right because God is on the scene, and when He is present, nothing is impossible. There is a trust, confidence; a knowing that can only be developed by going through the fire of affliction.

One person who had confidence was Jesus. He knew where He came from. He knew what He was sent to do, and where He was going. When you get to that level of confidence, of knowing God's plans and purpose for your life, you will not be moved by small things such as people's judgements and criticisms. You have this backed up faith, that you know who you belong to; you know God is only your side, you know that His Hand is upon your life. You know what He has called you to do, so you are not moved by anything. You know that He will help you reach the finish line because He knows the end from the beginning.

As a woman of authority, you need to know that you can do anything through the Holy Spirit. Without this confidence in God and knowing that through Him I can do all things, I would not stand in front of hundreds and talk about Jesus when I was once judged for talking about Him in high school.

One of the most confident women we find in the Bible is Queen Esther. She had quiet confidence which helped her find favour with the king. God honoured her, and the prayers the other Jews were praying, and the king received her warmly. In the end, Esther saved her people from perishing (Esther 5-10).

Too many times, having a fear of making mistakes stops one from trying out new things. Something about fear is that it brings a lack of confidence in God and you. Woman learn to replace your concerns with confidence. A confident woman is not afraid to try out new things without the fear of failing.

Whenever you feel afraid, always remember that God is with you. Study the Word and get to know God's character and nature. You will find that He can be relied on because He is trustworthy. You do not have to know how He will fulfil His promise or when He will fulfil it, but simply knowing He is with you, is more than enough of a reason. Woman know today that God is in control, and He knows what He is doing.

You may not see a way or do not think how God could pull you through for, but believe me, He has a way. It may look impossible to you, but God specialises in achieving what seems impossible to man. Woman, get up, dare to trust Him; He has never once failed before, and the good news is that He is not about to start now. God has you right in the palm of His hands; He is about to do something great for you; just put your confidence in Him.

PRAYER

Dear God, I focus on the truth - You are my refuge and strength. Help me to trust in You with all my heart and not to lean on my understanding. Teach me to acknowledge You in all my ways so that You can make my path straight. In you alone, I am completely confident. Amen.

CHAPTER 5

Be Strong

Philippians 4:13 - *"I can do all this through him who gives me strength."*

In the scripture above, Apostle Paul said this statement at a time when he was facing so many challenges in his life. Let me remind you of the things he went through. He spent the night on an open sea with no food, was shipwrecked, falsely accused and thrown into prison. He knew what he was saying when he said: "I can do all things through Him who gives me strength." He could have been bitter or discouraged, but he knew that God has already infused strength within him to overcome any challenge that may come his way. He was more than equipped for this battle.

The Apostle Paul got bitten by a snake right in front of a group on the island of Melita, the people who stayed there knew very well how venomous the particular snake was and so they probably expected him to swell up or fall. However, no, Paul just shook off the snake into the fire, and the Bible says he was unharmed (Acts 28:3-6). We all go through challenges, but when you encounter them, learn to handle it the way Paul did. He did not speak negatively when that snake bit him; he just shook off that kind of a negative mindset and refused to feel sorry for himself. Every morning you need to remind yourself that you are ready for anything that may come your way.

The scripture says in Matthew 5:45 that *"The rain falls on the just and the unjust."* When you decided to accept Jesus Christ as your Lord and Saviour, God never promised us that we would be exempt from difficulties. In the book of Matthew 24-27, Jesus told a parable about where one person who honoured God decided to build a house on a rock. Another person who did not honour God built his house on sand. The amazing thing is that the storm came to both people and the wind blew both their houses. The only difference is that when the storm comes, and you honour God, you will be able to stand. Why? Because God has given you the strength to overcome any challenge. Whatever situation you may find yourself in, know God gave it to you for a reason. He would not have allowed it if you could not handle it.

If you study the book of Genesis, in chapter 37 from verse 1-50, you will find the story of Joseph. Joseph was betrayed by his own brothers because he told them who God said he would be. They threw him into a pit, sold him into slavery and then to make matters worse, he spent years in prison for something he did not do. However, he did not get depressed or start complaining. He knew that God has already won this battle and given him the strength for it. In the end, God fulfilled His vision to him. One thing I have learned is that what is meant to harm you; God will use it to your advantage and let Himself be glorified. Whatever you may be going through, know that it will not defeat you but promote you.

I went through a situation where I was dismissed from the University of Pretoria due to poor performance. I tried to apply to various universities, but most of them would not take me because they required my academic transcript from my previous institution, and because my fees at the University of Pretoria were not paid in full, I could not submit my transcript in time. I honestly thought my school career was over. I had so many negative thoughts until I listened to a sermon by my spiritual father, Prophet Shepherd Bushiri. During that sermon, he spoke about how, even during the challenges he was facing at that time, he continually declared positive words upon his life. He did not go weary because he knew that he could do all things through Christ who has given him strength.

I decided to apply the same principle and began to go into prayer; I changed my mindset and confession. I started declaring what I wanted to see. I confessed out loud and every day that God will see me through. I am more than a conqueror. God has given me the strength already to triumph over this challenge. A week later, I got an email from the University of Johannesburg telling me that I have been accepted to come and study accounting at their institution. I was in shock because it is impossible to get accepted into another institution if they do not have your academic transcript and if your fees are not paid in full. Now, today as we speak, I am studying what I have always wanted to study.

Nothing can keep you from your destiny, no person and no disappointment. God has given you the strength to handle it. In those times, you are facing challenges that you feel are overwhelming you; always remember that nothing is a surprise to God.

Labour pain, according to research, is one of the most severe pains which has ever been evaluated. Now, imagine the type of strength God has infused in you as a woman. You are much stronger than a man physically, although they may look bigger, you are stronger than them. If you can survive pains like labour and period, how much more other challenges. Whatever you may be going through, remember that God is in complete control. You do not have to get angry or bitter when things do not go according to how you planned. God has given you the power to remain calm, utilise it. Prophet Isaiah says in the scriptures that *"Take hold of His strength"* (Isaiah 27:5). When you tell yourself that God has given you the strength to handle anything that comes your way, you are taking hold of His strength. That is why the scripture in Joel 3:10 says, *"Let the weak say, I am strong."*

Philippians 1: 28, says, *"Do not be intimidated by your enemies."* Woman get up and do not be intimidated by that problem; God says He has you in the palm of His hands. God, who is more powerful than any other opposition, and His Word say that He lives in you. You can handle any challenge that comes your way.

There was a time when I was on the right track, serving God, doing well at school. Then one night when I was driving on my way home on the highway, there was a line of rocks out on the middle of the road. I did not see them from afar as I was travelling at a very high speed. I bumped into the rocks and got a puncher, so I could not move my car any further as I got out to have a look at what exactly was going on. A group of men came out of the bushes holding guns and forced me into the forest. They took my phone, laptop and money. I was filled with so much fear; I was praying the whole time for them not to rape me or worse even kill me. In the end, those people did not also lay a hand on me; they were even asking me if my car was fine and would be able to drive back home. I could have got discouraged and went into depression, but I knew that God has infused strength within me and that I am strong in Him. Two days later, my biological father got involved in a car accident; it was a hit and run. I was shattered, but I knew that higher is He that is in me than He that is in the world. The strength you develop when you know that your God is unimaginable is amazing.

As a woman of authority, you should know that you have already been given the strength to face and overcome every challenge that may come your way. God has not only given you the strength to make it through, but to come out better than before. Had I not gone through all those challenges; I would not have a story to tell neither would I be as strong as I am today. Woman, regardless of whatever you went through, what matters is that God never left you nor forsook you. Look at how stronger you are today; look at how your faith has grown and how mature you are now. God brought you this far for a reason, and He is still taking you farther. You are strong enough to overcome anything that comes your way, even when you feel weak. God, the most powerful source, is on your side; no force of darkness can stop you.

PRAYER

Dear God, thank You that You have already overcome every enemy. Thank You for the strength You have infused in me for every obstacle that will come my way, in Jesus' name. I pray. Amen.

CHAPTER 6

Be secure

Romans 8:29 - *"For those whom He foreknew [and loved and chose beforehand], He also predestined to be conformed to the image of His Son [and ultimately share in His complete sanctification], so that He would be the firstborn [the most beloved and honoured] among believers."*

The scripture above says that we are destined to be moulded into the image of Jesus Christ and share inwardly in His likeness. The Bible tells us in Philippians 2 that we have the mind of Christ. When one has the mind of Christ, it simply means we can think, speak and learn to behave as He did. One thing about Jesus is that He never compared Himself with anyone or desire to be anything other than what His Father made Him be. Jesus lived all His life to do precisely His Father's will; He did not compete with others or compare Himself. We can look up to people, they can be examples for us, but they should never be our standard or a reason for us to yearn to be exactly like them.

I have heard a saying that says, "Comparison, is a thief of joy." Woman, as long as you keep comparing yourself to others, you will never feel good about yourself. There will always be someone more beautiful, successful, and talented than you. That should not discourage you; you should know you have your race to run. God has given you a specific assignment that can only be fulfilled by you. God has not only given you an assignment, but He has also given you everything that you need to accomplish that assignment. You have to focus and stop comparing yourself to others. Woman get up and focus!

In 1954, the famous story of the race between Bannister and Landy, both outstanding athletes. Landy was leading in their race, but he looked back on his left to see how far Bannister was. At that very moment, Bannister came by on his right and won the race. Had Landy, just focused on his own race and did not compare himself to Bannister he would have won. That is precisely what comparison does; it only delays you and takes your eyes off your race. Stop comparing yourself and focus on your race!

I have seen in many instances, that we often try to pursue titles, thinking that once we have obtained such titles, we will feel good about ourselves. I admit that I am guilty of that too. I always used to tell myself that I could not write a book or preach about Jesus because there are specific titles, such as being an accountant that I have not achieved. I thought to myself, what would I say to people if I could not even obtain that degree. God then told me one day that I do not need a title to do what He has called me to do. As a woman of authority do not wait for people to approve you or validate you. Use the gift that God has given you, and the title will come; there is no need to rush.

If a great man from the Bible called King David had waited for a title to do what God has called him to do, we would not have a story to tell about him. When David was sent by God to face Goliath, he was not qualified or a sergeant. A title could not stop him; David still went out and defeated Goliath (1 Samuel 17). A few years later, after he had defeated Goliath, he was given the title: "King of Israel". Learn to use the God-given gifts and the titles will always follow you.

You should first learn to accept the gift God gave you. Whether it is the gift of writing, the gift of playing tennis or the gift of singing, learn to accept that gift. You should not have to feel small or inferior if someone else seems to have a more meaningful gift. It takes a person who is secure and has the authority to say, "I'm comfortable with who God created me to be."

I used to play a sport called Drum Majorettes; I was extremely good at it as I was in the national team. I was a leader for my team, and during competitions, I would see other leaders from various teams. They would move the crowd with their new dresses. They were tall, had the strength and were flexible, which worked out best, and I would stand up in front of the crowd as short as I am. But this is what God gave me; I could not change how I looked. I could, however, improve and develop my routine, but I was never going to look exactly like them. One thing I learned from that was that there will always be somebody better and someone who is more experienced than me. But you know what? That did not bother me. I knew God had given me the gifts that I needed for my assignment.

Woman, God has given you a gift, quit discounting it. Your gift may seem insignificant when you compare it to someone else's but what He has given you is unique; it is something that will take you into your destiny.

The scriptures talk about how we should consider it pure joy when we face various trials and tribulations (James 1:2-4). Another version tells us that God has given us the power to enjoy whatever may be thrown at us, which means that I do not have the grace or power to enjoy another person's life. God has only given me the power to enjoy my life. Another person, may be more successful, much smarter, have more money and more beautiful, but if God had to put you in her life, you would not enjoy it. God has uniquely designed us to run our own race. We would not be tempted to compare ourselves if we truly understood and embraced this. Instead, we should take God has already given you and develop it. Learn to make the most of it. The life God has given you is perfectly matched for you.

An example of someone who compared himself and did not focus on his race was King Saul. He lost the throne because he heard women saying that he had only killed thousands, while David has killed ten thousand (1 Samuel 18:7). From that day, he never looked at David the same way; he started comparing himself and thought that David could not outperform him. He could not handle somebody else getting ahead of him. He got distracted, stopped running his race and spent months trying to kill David all because he was not comfortable with whom he was.

You have to learn to get excited about you who you are, how you look, your personality and talent. If you would not celebrate yourself, no one will. Learn to be secure with yourself. Insecurity is stealing the joy of life from many people and causing significant problems in their lives. Insecurity has a terrible effect on one's life; I know this because I experienced it. I know how one feels and what it does to a person. Insecure people often seek approval from others; they are approval addicts because they are trying to overcome their feelings of rejection and low self-esteem. There is only one thing that will set us free, and that is God's truth. God's truth never changes, His truth is that we do not need to struggle to get from man what He freely gives us and that is: love, acceptance, approval, worth, and the list goes on.

One of the best things I have learned is to be comfortable and secure with whom God made me be. I know that I do not have to compete or try to outperform anyone to feel good about myself. I am busy running my own race. Woman do not compare yourself but celebrate yourself. Remember that it is about becoming who God made you be and not anyone else. One thing about God is that He will never help you be someone else. Get up and run your race!

PRAYER

Dear God, thank You for the unique way You have created me. I look to You for security. I focus on the truth. You give me love and acceptance. Thank You that I am fearfully and wonderfully made. Today I choose not to compare myself with anyone, and I choose to celebrate people who pass me by. Amen.

CHAPTER 7

A Heart of Gratitude Builds

1 Corinthians 10:9-10 - *"We should not tempt the Lord [try His patience, become a trial to Him, critically appraise Him, and exploit His goodness] as some of them did — and were killed by poisonous serpents; nor discontentedly complain as some of them did- and were out of the way entirely by the destroyer (death)."*

The scripture above refers to the time when the Israelites spoke against God and Moses (Numbers 21:5-6). They were murmuring and complaining, which is something God does not want us to do. Notice that when you complain and murmur, you only expose yourself to snares, danger and temptations. The Israelites tempted and spoke against God (they complained) this resulted in them getting bitten, leading most of them to death.

As a woman, you know that you should be grateful for your many blessings; you do not need to be continuously reminded. God tells us in His Word to be thankful, a matter of a fact; He tells us to give thanks in all circumstances. Once you start seriously to provide God with praise, the burden and trouble always seem to weigh less heavily on your shoulders.

I remember when I wrote my final examination in my third year. It was a second examination; meaning after this exam, there would be no more chances. I begged for a remark, but they refused; I was disappointed and heartbroken. That Sunday it was a Thanksgiving Sunday at church, so we spent the whole day at church worshipping, no teaching, no praying, but thanking God in advance for the things He was going to do in our lives and all that He had already done. The following day, some students and I were called to come and collect our examination scripts.

I think I was one of the last few people to go and collect my script. As I walked in and signed for my paper, my lecturer told me the most amazing and unbelievable news. He told me that they had found extra marks on my examination paper for that specific module, which caused me to pass the module. I was shocked and could not believe what I heard. The situation sounded impossible because there was no way that a lecturer could go back to my paper after weeks, without applying for a remark. I then remembered how I spent my previous Sunday, thanking God. Woman, there is power in thanksgiving. When you give God praise, God steps in to fight your battles.

One mistake that the Israelites did was that every time something did not go well for them, they would complain and exploit God's goodness. Every time we do not open our mouths to give thanks to God, we are only exploiting His goodness.

Woman do not be known as a person who is always complaining.

Can you imagine if you had to always complain to your husband or boyfriend, how do you think that makes him feel? Be confident of the fact that God is still in control no matter what is going on in your life or what mess you have found yourself in. Be known as a woman who has a heart of gratitude and learn to give God thanks all the time.

Being thankful means having the kind of heart that is sensitive to God's working in our everyday lives. It means that every time we see God working in our lives, we cannot help but breathe out prayers of thanksgiving. It comes; naturally, we do not have to sit down and force ourselves to try to remember what we need to be grateful for to make God happy.

When we complain and murmur, we open up so many doors for the devil in our lives. When you ask God for something, and He gives it to you, how many times have you complained that you have to take care of it? This is the kind of wilderness mentality that keeps us from living in the Promised Land that God destined for us. In Philippians 2:14, we are told to do "all things" without complaining – notice how it says all things and not some things. Woman, you should learn to thank God when things are going right, and when things are wrong.

One thing about God is that He loves to be worshipped. God goes out of His way to seek a worshipper. When He finds a worshipper, there is nothing He would not do for that person. He said in His Word, *"I will seek for me a man after my own heart"* (1 Samuel 13:14; Acts 13:22). The highest form of reaching God is in worship. My spiritual Father always tells us that in Heaven, God is surrounded by worshippers (angels) and not complainers. This means God wants to hear people praising Him all the time and not complaining; hence, why He could get so upset at the Israelites when they were protesting in the wilderness. God created us to worship Him. God can do everything, but there is only one thing He cannot do, and that is worship Himself.

David was a worshipper. David's wife looked through the window and despised David in her heart. God took it personally and closed her womb (2 Samuel 6:12-23). You cannot touch a worshipper and expect God not to react.

When Job encountered a series of calamities in his life, he fell and worshipped God. At the highest and lowest points of his life, Job still worshipped. The revelation that he got before his trial is what sustained him. He knew the temptation came because God was proud of Him (Job 1-3). You are never tempted for anything, but God is out to prove something. Paul tells us in the book of Thessalonians to encourage one another. To encourage means to support, cheer or hope to someone. This is something that God wants us to do as women.

Women, unlike men, are more sensitive to the needs of others. I believe God that when He created you and me, He gave us the ability to help other people with their infirmities. Jesus told us in Matthew 16:24 that if we want to be His disciples, we should forget about ourselves and follow Him. Everything you do for other people, according to the Word of God in Luke 6:3, will come back to you with joy, many times over.

When you are willing to give yourself away, help and encourage other people, you are guaranteed to have a much better life and feel more fulfilled than you ever would have if you try to keep yourself. That is the basis of Christianity, love. You cannot love without giving. While we are running our race, we all encounter difficulty and always need encouragement. The more encouragement we get, the fewer days we waste being in depression and the more focused we are. God in His Word teaches us to sow, and then we shall reap. If you want to receive something, learn to give more. Encourage others, and you will always be encouraged.

Refuse to be the kind of person that only takes in life and never adds anything. Be a woman that makes other people's lives better. Do not be selfish in this life but do everything you can to help as often as you can. Be a woman that empowers, that edifies that lifts up, and that gives hope and encourage other women. Be the type of woman that God can use to keep someone going and achieving their goals.

Joel Osteen said something profound; "Encouragement to others is something everyone can give. Someone needs what you have to give. It may not be your money; it may be your time. It may be your listening ear. It may be your arms to encourage. It may be your smile to uplift. Who knows?"

As a woman of authority, learn to sow seeds of encouragement to others, and you will reap those same seeds in your lives.

PRAYER

Dear God, help me to be a woman that builds other people up. Help me to stop complaining and let me see all the beautiful things You are doing in my life. I thank You for everything, and I thank You in advance for all the great things You will do, in Jesus' Mighty Name, I pray. Amen.

CHAPTER 8

Be content

Philippians 4:12 - *"In any and all circumstances, I have learned the secret of being content — whether well fed or hungry, whether in abundance or in need."*

Notice how the Apostle Paul says in the above scripture that he had to learn to be content. It is not something that came automatically to him; he had to choose to be content.

Content, according to the Oxford Dictionary, means that you are in a state of peaceful happiness. One thing about being content is that you are not frustrated. It does not mean we do not want change or that we settle where we are. Being content means that you trust God's timing, and you know that He would get us to where we are destined to be at the right time.

We should not be discontent while we are waiting for things to change in our lives. Woman learn to enjoy the season that you are in currently. We dishonour God when we are discontent because we are not grateful for what we already have. Contentment is learning how to be happy with what you have already been blessed with.

One of the most valuable lessons we can learn is from the story of David. David was chosen and anointed by the prophet Samuel to be the next king of Israel. However, he spent years taking care of his father's sheep. A lot was probably going on through David's head at that time; he could have thought to himself that what was going on was not right and not part of God's plan.

However, David understood what it means to be content. He was confident and knew that God was in control, so he just continued going to work as usual. He knew that God would fulfil his promise to him. Eventually, he became the king of Israel just as God promised.

Woman, learn to be content in the season you are in. While you are waiting for your story to change, learn to be content in your current season. Do not let your contentment be based on who likes you or on what you have. When you always wish for something different or what someone else has, you will still be unhappy. A mistake that we often make is that we think that we will only be happy when we reach a particular goal.
The reason some people are worn out is that they are continually trying to impress and compete with others. When you live in such a way where you are always trying to prove to someone that you are better, it is like you are on a treadmill. As soon as you have proven to one person that you are making it and everything is still on track, you will see someone else you

need to impress and prove a point. That cycle never ends. Woman get up and get off that treadmill! You are wasting your time, working hard, and it is leading you nowhere.

While I was still in high school, I always used to say I cannot wait until I finish my matric and go to university. Joel Osteen on Twitter once said, "With every blessing comes a burden." When I reached university, I encountered many more problems, and I was even more discontent. One lesson I learned from all of that is that I should learn to be content with where I am or else, I would not also be satisfied when my dreams come to pass.

Paul said in 1 Timothy 6:6 that "Godliness accompanied with contentment (that contentment, which is a sense of inward sufficiency) is great and abundant gain." When you choose to be content in the Lord, it truly makes you happy. When you can say to God that you only want what He wants for you, will bring you so much peace and happiness.

As a woman of authority, you should learn to be content. Understand that God's plan for our life is not to make us comfortable but to grow us, to mature us. You may not like where you are but accept it and learn that God has a purpose for your life.

PRAYER
Dear God, I only want what You want for me. Like the Apostle Paul, I choose to be content in every circumstance, in Jesus' name. I pray. Amen.

CHAPTER 9

You are forgiven

Isaiah 43: 25-26 - *"I, even I, am He who blots out and cancels your transgressions, for My own sake, and I will not remember your sins. Put Me in remembrance [remind Me of your merits]; let us plead and argue together. Set forth your case, that you may be justified (proved right)."*

In the scripture above, regardless of all the sins, the children of Israel had committed against God, He still chose to forgive them. The scripture tells us that God forgives and forgets and that He will not remember the sins of His people against them. Prophet Isaiah reminds us that God holds nothing against us. When you trust in the blood of Jesus to cleanse you, and you are sincerely sorry for what you have done, God will not hold anything against you.

I used to think that God only loves me when I am doing the right thing and not sinning, but the problem is that we all make mistakes. The truth is that God created us to love and not punish us. God is love and only executes love. The Bible tells in 1 John 4:16 tells us that we are the objects of His love; He created us especially to love us. Can you even comprehend that thought?

The day I realised that God, who is love, made me so that He can love changed my life forever. It did not matter who rejected me or turned on me; all that matters was that God loves me. We can never love God or people if we do not know how much He truly loves us. I pray today that you lean on the fact that God loves you, and you gain freedom from your past hurts.

One thing you should know about God's character is that when you fall, He does not turn His back away from you. Instead, He chooses to come after you and show you that He is on your side. Do not be so hard on yourself when you are not always perfect or do things correctly; God loves imperfect people. Think about the story of Peter; Jesus knew every mistake he would make; he knew Peter would deny Him. He still chose him to be one of his disciples. God knows every mistake we will ever make, but His love for us is not based on our performance; hence, He still chooses us.

In Luke 22:61, Peter denied Jesus, not once but three times and the rooster crowed. Peter's eyes met with Jesus, right after he had just denied knowing him. The scriptures tell us, "Peter went out and wept bitterly." You can imagine how he felt. When Jesus was at His lowest, when He needed a friend, when He needed someone to be there for Him, Peter denied Him. Three days after Jesus' death, Mary Magdalene went to the tomb to check on His body and found that the stone was rolled away. It says in Mark 16:6-14 that an angel appeared to her and said *"Mary, don't be afraid. Jesus is not here. He is risen. Now go tell His disciples and Peter than He is alive."*

Out of all the disciples and everyone one in the world, God correctly pointed out Peter. God was saying to Peter that He is not upset at him, and He has forgiven him. He was reminding him that even when he falls, He would always be there to pick him up.

We have all made some horrible choices in life, but do not let that heaviness or guilt weigh you down and keep you from seeing what God has in store for you. Woman, you should know the minute you ask God to forgive you. He has already done that and has not cancelled your destiny.

I remember, at some point in 2018; I was not enjoying my life due to the series of choices I had made. This resulted in me feeling that everything I did require so much effort and produced such little reward. I went through a lot of disappointments and pain. Throughout this period, I learned that the only solution was to make the right decisions and stop thinking about all the wrong ones I made.

One thing I have learned is that if you want to walk out of trouble or a bad situation, you have to do the opposite of what got you into that trouble in the first place. Start making the right choices. Most of the time, you find that the bad results happening in your life are because of the bad decisions you made. You may be failing in school because you never attend class or study. You may be in debt because you made bad decisions with your money or squandered it. You may be lonely because of how you treat people or the bad choices you made in your previous relationships. You may be overweight or sick because you do not eat healthily or exercise.

It is like the principle of sowing and reaping. You cannot make so many bad decisions that result in you in problems and then make one good decision and expect everything to go right and erase all your bad choices. You do not find yourself in trouble because of one wrong choice you make but plenty. If you want your life to change for the better, you need to start by making the right decisions.

The Bible tells us to forget the former things and not to dwell on the past. You cannot do anything about what has happened, but what you can do is focus on your future and what lies ahead. No matter what type of situation you find yourself in, you can find a way and still have a good life.

When someone hurts us, we feel as though they owe us, and we often want to get revenge. However, God does not wish to that; He wants us to let go. God wants us to forgive; if we do not forgive why He should forgive us? He knows our worst flaws, but still chooses to forgive us.

The problem is that when you do not forgive, it makes you bitter; when you go around being angry with that person, thinking it is hurting them. You are just hindering yourself because it hurts you more than it hurts them. Bitterness is drinking poison, and thinking it is going to kill the other person. Bitterness is saying, "Well, I will just hold on to this, and they will be sorry for what they did." Well, unfortunately, it is not like that, they are walking around fine and sleeping well at night while you are tossing and turning and your relationships are not working. God is saying the reason you cannot get free is that you will not forgive.
Satan often perpetuates the greatest deception that if our feelings have not changed towards that person, we have not forgiven them. But that is a lie; do not let the devil deceive you and convince you that because your feelings have not changed that you have not forgiven that person.

You could have decided to forgive that person, and your feelings have not changed, but that is where faith comes in. You have done your part, forgiven them as God told you to; now let God do His part and heal your emotions and change your feelings towards the person who hurt you.

A woman of authority does not live in the past; she lets go and looks to the future. Woman accept the mercy of God and know that your sins have already been forgiven. God has paid every sin and mistake for you in full. Do not go around feeling guilty about the mistakes you have done. Move on. God knew every mistake you would make and does not love you any less. He is still rooted in love with you.

PRAYER

Dear God, thank You for forgiving me; I accept Your forgiveness. I choose to forgive those who hurt me. I release them from their debt in Jesus' name. Heal my heart and make me whole. Amen.

CHAPTER 10

Be determined to finish

1 Corinthians 9:24-25 - *"Do you not know that in a race all the runners compete, but [only] one receives the prize? So, run [your race] that you may lay hold [of the prize] and make it yours. Now every athlete who goes into training conducts himself temperately and restricts himself in all things. We do [do it to receive a crown of eternal blessedness] that cannot wither."*

In the scripture above, Paul chooses an athletic metaphor to illustrate his point. Just as an athlete must practise making it possible for her to win a race, so also Christians must practise individual discipline to make it possible for them to win the spiritual prize. In a race, you usually focus on yourself, and you run at your own pace to finish and win the prize. Paul tells us to run in such a way that we may win.

I have noticed that it is so easy to start something and usually does not require a lot of effort, but finishing is what is challenging. The Word of God tells us that He is the author and finisher of our faith. Something about God is that he gives us the grace to start and the grace to finish. Woman, you were not created to quit, so do not give up. Get and finish your race. You have been given the grace to finish.

You may have a dream, and it is taking slightly longer to come to pass, do not give up on that dream. That is what the enemy wants you to do. He does not have a problem with you starting, but once he sees that you have made up your mind and you are determined to see your dream come to pass, that is when he tries all means to stop you from finishing. He will try and throw any obstacles that he can think of your way.

I remember the time when I was robbed and mugged at gunpoint; it was after I had announced on social media that my book would be coming out soon. The day when that incident happened, I had planned to have so many meetings that day with regards to my book launch; I was delayed by this terrible incident that happened to me. As soon as I tried to get back on my feet and continue with my life and the book launch, my dad got involved in a car accident, and therefore, I could not do all that I desired to do. The enemy saw I was close to finishing and that caught his attention; hence, he threw all kinds of obstacles my way to stop me from finishing. However, he forgot that I serve a living God.

It says in Philippians that *"God began a good work in you, and He will continue to perform it until it is complete"* (Philippians 1:6). Another translation with the same verse says, *"He will bring you to a flourishing finish."*

Notice how the Bible is not talking about a finish where we are barely making it, or where we are ultimately defeated. Apostle Paul said that He would finish your race with you. God has given you the grace to complete your assignment and become everything that He destined you to become. Your finish will not be one where you are beaten up and not be able to continue, but it shall be a flourishing one.

God gave Joseph a dream that he would rule the nation. Joseph told his brothers what God say he would be. His brothers could not handle it and became extremely jealous of him. They sold him into slavery. Joseph had not done anything wrong. He could have got discouraged, depressed and bitter and thought that his dream would not come to pass. However, Joseph understood that the same God who gave him that dream would ensure that it comes to pass. He knew that he was headed in the right direction because the enemy would not have been fighting him if he were not (Genesis 37).

One day Pharaoh has a dream and the only person who could interpret it was Joseph (Genesis 41). The dream that God gave Joseph finally came to pass. What God has put inside of you will override anything or anyone that comes against you.

Apostle Paul was arrested and put in prison for something he did not do. Paul could have got discouraged and felt sorry for himself. But the opposite happened even though he was in chains. Prison gates could not stop him from doing what God called him to do. He wrote over half of the New Testament since he could not go out and preach the Word of God to thousands. He wrote much of the New Testament in prison. The enemy though, was stopping him; but God used what was meant to harm him, for his own good.

Paul came to the end of his life and said, *"I finished my course with joy"* (2 Timothy 4:7) Paul did not finish his race bitter and depressed; he ended it with a smile. Woman, this is how God wants you to complete your race. With a big smile!

The people who try to discredit and stop you are all part of the plan to get you to your finished line. Do not let them upset you. God will use such people to move you forward. Jehovah has the final say. If he could bring Joseph out of prison, what is your situation?

Paul and Joseph were both in prison, but they fulfilled their destinies. You may go through some things that pull you back, do not worry. That situation is not permanent but only temporary. It is all part of the plan to your destiny.

God says that we are victorious. He has set me free from many addictions and sins. I may still have some battles that I need to win, but the great thing is that I am already victorious. Woman, I encourage you to think about something that you would like to start working on. Your next step is to think about your victory. Think about all the positive things and how your life will be once you have been set free.

As a woman of authority, you should be determined to finish your race. Know that the same God who gave you the grace to start is the same God who will provide you with the grace to finish. Make a decision today to get up and finish your race with joy.

PRAYER
Dear God, thank You for the grace to start and finish my race. May I finish it with joy, in Jesus' name, I pray. Amen.

CHAPTER 11

Be prayerful

1 Thessalonians 5:17- _"Pray without ceasing."_

In all the years that I have lived, I have discovered that there is one thing that is of utmost importance in any believer's life and that is prayer. It may seem simple and is often overlooked, but I can never stress enough the importance and essentiality of remaining prayerful.

When we talk about prayer, we seek to describe a process whereby you are given the opportunity not only to speak to God but experience Him talking right back at you. Prayer is our way of linking what is in the natural with that, which is supernatural. Through prayer, we experience tangible changes in our lives and through the very same prayer, we can experience heaven here on earth.

Therefore, when the Bible says to _"pray continually"_ or _"to pray without ceasing"_ (1 Thessalonians 5:17) it seeks to emphasise what I have just been narrating above.

Prayer is not supposed to be circumstantial; that is, prayer is not supposed to be done only when one feels like it. Instead, it is supposed to be done continuously, without tiring, hesitation or even reluctance. Prayer ought to be so frequent just as breathing!

You need to get to a point in your life where prayer ceases to be a habit or a hobby but rather, a lifestyle. It should come naturally to you. It is important to note that the scripture in Thessalonians does not mean that we do nothing all day except pray, but it does make the point that prayer ought to be our central defining point as children of God.

Whenever we set out hearts in prayer, we bring our desires and wishes before the Lord. And once this is done, we challenge Him to answer us. No one can fulfil your requests; only God can. If you need promotion, only God can grant it. If you need a baby or a partner in life, only God can supply. And if you need a financial reward, best believe that God can. Everything comes from God, and everything belongs to God. Talk to Him in prayer; He is more than willing to listen and give you what you need.

Now, narrowing it down to you, woman, take note that prayer is essential for a woman with authority. When you pray more, you talk less. Failure to lead a prayerful life can birth out a particular weakness like foolish talk. As my mother in the Lord, Prophetess Mary Bushiri always says, "When you do not know what to do with the raging battle, pray." One thing I love about prayer is that it is a gift from God to humankind. God even sent His Holy Spirit to make things easier for us. The Holy Spirit is continually interceding and praying on our behalf.

Now, imagine the Creator of the universe is taking time to hear what you have to say to Him. The scriptures even say that God is mindful of us (Psalms 8:4; 115:12) Also, Jesus often took time to pray to His Father; He did nothing without letting His Father aware.

In the book of Luke chapter 6, it says that Jesus went to the mountain and prayed all night. He prayed without ceasing. Through prayer, we can get all the answers we need in life; we even develop a sense of peace. Prayer opens the door for God to work in our lives, situations, and the lives of our loved ones.

I remember during my matric year in 2015, I had applied to various universities. My first option was Wits University, and I got provisionally accepted. However, the University of Pretoria had rejected my acceptance letter, which means, I was completely scratched off from their system. At the beginning of 2016, when I got my matric results, I was waiting for a response from Wits University. I was receiving responses from other universities telling me that I could come to study with them. But my heart was not there; I wanted to go to Wits so that I could attend church.

One night I decided to check my Wits application status, and I got the shock of my life when I saw it, for it said I was rejected. I kept quiet and did not tell my family; I spent the whole night praying and crying out to God. I gave God all the reasons why I wanted to be in Gauteng province. The following day, my father decided to call the University of Pretoria. He spoke to a lady who then explained that my name was not on the system as I was rejected for what I applied for, but she would put me on a course at the University of Pretoria. From that day, I was accepted to the University of Pretoria. Bear in mind; I was already a week late. My father came back and told my family the fantastic news. It was then I told them that Wits rejected me.

The following day, my father called the same number, asking to speak to the same lady, as we wanted more information. However, we were told nobody by that name worked in that office. We were all shocked, but that is what the power of prayer can do.

I have seen prayer opening doors for me. I have seen prayer moving mountains that stood in my stead. I have seen prayer provoking God to do the impossible for me. He is faithful to those that make an effort to seek Him in prayer. If you are reading this right now, I want to encourage you to remain a prayerful woman. Just like Hannah (1 Samuel 1:10), when you stay persistent in prayer, you will see God removing your shame and giving you a miracle that the entire nation will celebrate. Like Prophetess Anna (Luke 2:36-38), when you remain in prayer, you will see God exalting you even in hopeless situations.

PRAYER

Dear God, thank You for giving me prayer as a gift that I can use to communicate with You. As you raise me, help me to be able to have a prayerful life. May I never seek to speak to anyone before I talk to You. In good and bad times, help me to continue praying without ceasing, in Jesus' Name, I pray. Amen.

Conclusion

I have shared much of my personal experiences here. I have tried to shed light on many truths that I have either stumbled across, learnt painful lessons and been graced to absorb in my journey. As I sit here, reflecting my prayer, more than publishing, my thoughts and experiences in a book are more than that. This testimony should help you change your life. I have touched on many subjects, which are Christ centred, based on the teachings I am privy to at Enlightened Christian Gathering. I have given hints and pointers to key areas which require our attention and will help the ordinary woman reach that place of peace we all love, where our relationship with God and man is perfectly balanced, and we are impacting our generation. I am excited with what God is doing, and I am filled with passion and the Holy Ghost, ready for the great adventure that lies ahead. I wish I could say I leave you well, but that is not my intention at all. I hope that, as I launch into the vast and many adventures of ministry, you too will get up and get going! That is the next step: get going.

Do not get up and be a pew warmer or another young person who says she knows Jesus. Go and get the world ready for Jesus! Whether you take off in a jet or start in a taxi or share with your roommate or family member, it does not matter. What is important is that you get up and get the ball moving!

Do not look down at yourself, forgive yourself, God already did. Love yourself and submit to God. Acknowledge and learn from your mistakes. Make sure you hold on to Jesus firmly as you get up; whatever you do woman, get up!

www.ingramcontent.com/pod-product-compliance
Lightning Source LLC
Chambersburg PA
CBHW031328060726
47590CB00003B/1369